She's Beautiful Inside & Out
A celebration of self-love and kindness

To Amy,
You're loved, kind, and loved!
Love,
Merlynne.T

Written by: **Merlynne Tuwizana**
Illustrated by: **Le Rêve London**

To Amy,
You're loved, kind, and loved!
Love,
Jerhyme T.
M

Copyright © 2024 by Merlynne Tuwizana
ISBN: 979-8-3392-9127-5
Published by Merlynne Tuwizana
Printed in the United Kingdom

All rights reserved. No part of this publication may be reproduced, stored in a retrieval system, or transmitted in any form or by any means electronic, mechanical, photocopying, recording, or otherwise without the prior written permission of the publisher. This publication contains original content and licensed elements. All materials are protected under international copyright laws. Unauthorised use of any part of this publication is strictly prohibited.
Available in multiple languages.

For more information, visit:
www.merlynnewrites.com

Dedicated to My Beloved Parents, Beatrice and Paul. Though you are no longer here, your love and guidance continue to inspire me every day. You are forever in my heart, and your legacy lives on through every word I write.

With all my love,
Merlynne

Dear Reader,

She's Beautiful Inside & Out is a heartwarming children's book designed to inspire young readers to embrace both their inner and outer beauty. Through positive affirmations and charming illustrations, this story encourages self-love, kindness, and confidence, reminding every child that they are truly beautiful just the way they are.

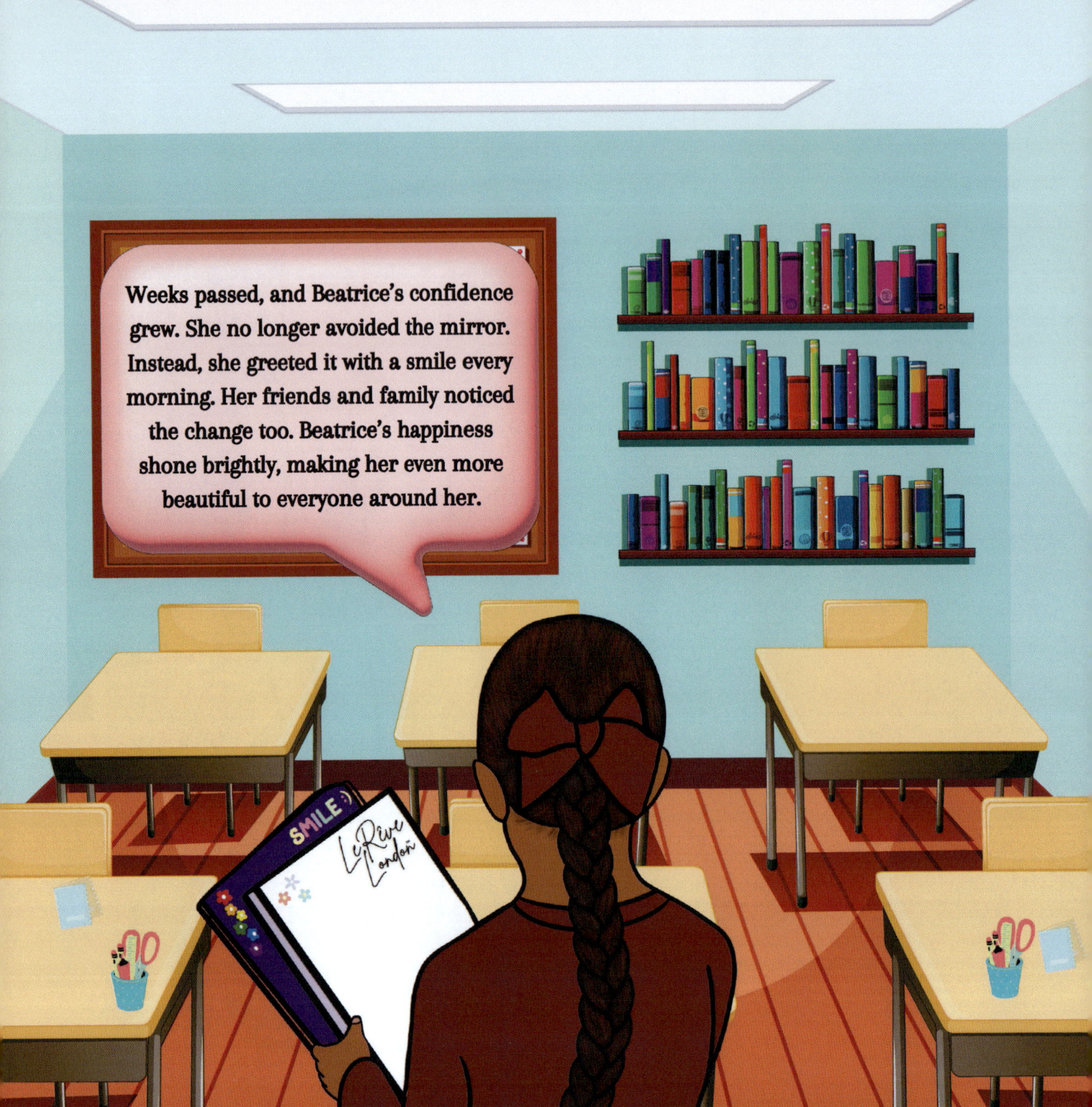

Stay Connected With Us!

Thank you so much for choosing She's Beautiful Inside & Out! As a self-published author, your support truly means the world to me. I poured my heart into this story, and I hope it has brought joy, love, and inspiration to you and the special children in your life.

If this book touched your heart, I'd love to hear your thoughts or see how it made an impact. Whether it's a favourite part, a shared moment with a loved one, or simply your reflections, don't hesitate to share and tag us on social media. We love connecting with our readers!

Instagram: @merlynnewrites / @lerevelondon
TikTok: @merlynnewrites / @lerevelondon
Facebook: @merlynnewrites / @lerevelondon

Why Stay Connected?

By following along, you'll be the first to hear about exciting new releases, special offers, and giveaways. You are helping make my dream of self-publishing a reality, and for that, I am forever grateful.

Together, we can continue spreading love, kindness, and self-confidence through stories.

Thank you for being part of this journey, it wouldn't be the same without you!

www.merlynnewrites.com

A Special Message To My Readers

I hope you enjoyed reading She's Beautiful Inside & Out! Beatrice's journey to self-love and kindness is one that we all can relate to, and I'd love to hear how the story has inspired you!

If you'd like to share your thoughts, write me a letter, or draw a picture of your favourite part of the story, I'd be thrilled to see it!

You can send your messages and artwork to:
Email: Contact@merlynnewrites.com

Thank you for joining Beatrice on her adventure. Remember, you are beautiful inside and out, just like her!

About The Author & Illustrator

Merlynne Tuwizana is the author and illustrator of She's Beautiful Inside & Out. Inspired by her passion for self-love and empowerment, she creates heartwarming stories that help children discover their inner beauty and build confidence. Through her books, Merlynne encourages young readers to believe in themselves and embrace the power of kindness and positive affirmations.

Visit www.merlynnewrites.com to read more about Merlynne's journey and her inspiring mission!

Printed in Great Britain
by Amazon